Contrary Visions

Scripta humanistica

Directed by
BRUNO M. DAMIANI
The Catholic University of America

ADVISORY BOARD

Contrary Visions

Carolyn Kreiter-Kurylo

𝔖cripta 𝔥umanistica

41

Kreiter-Kurylo, Carolyn.
    Contrary Visions / Carolyn Kreiter-Kurylo.
       p. cm. — (Scripta Humanistica; 41)
    ISBN 0-916379-47-7
    I. Title. II. Series: Scripta Humanistica (Series); 41.
PS3561.R395C6   1988
811'.54—dc19   87-27206

Publisher and Distributor:
SCRIPTA HUMANISTICA
1383 Kersey Lane
Potomac, Maryland 20854 U.S.A.

Printed in the United States of America

*It is with gratitude that I acknowledge the Virginia Commission
for the Arts' generous grant support of this book. I thank the
Commission also for an Artist-in-Education Study Grant sup-
porting my work as a poet in the schools.*

for my family
and for Peter and Irene

It is the beginning of a painting,
a piece of sculpture, or poem, or monument
. . . . Watch it closely.

Elizabeth Bishop
"The Monument"

Contents

Acknowledgments

The author wishes to express grateful appreciation to the editors of the following periodicals in which these poems, or earlier versions of them, first appeared.

Antioch Review:	"From a Café Window, Tangier"
Beacon Review:	"In the Bois de Vincennes, Paris" (originally published under the title, "In the Bois de Boulogne, Paris")
Best New Poets of 1986:	"Touching a Stained-Glass Window in Gloucester Cathedral"
Card Party:	"The Mathematical Bridge, Cambridge"
Day Tonight/Night Today:	"Other Possibilities"
The English Journal:	"A Former Teacher Said It Is Not Easy"
The Federal Poet:	"The Blind Woman, 1967"
Groundswell:	"Mountains"
Mid-American Review:	"The Replica"
Montpelier Plus 4 1980-1984:	"Donna Bruna"
Negative Capability:	"Take This on Authority"
New CollAge Magazine:	"The Waters of Bath"
Passages North:	"Crows over the Fields of Auvers"
Phoebe:	"Contrary Visions in the Gallery: *White on White*"
	"To Walk Out on Three Musicians"
	"20th Century Studio Scene"

	"The Enchantress"
	"Painting Poppies near Arles"
	"Proctoscopic Humiliation"
	"Gifts"
Poet Lore:	"What You Hear in a Studio"
	"The Peasant Woman above Tarifa"
	"Lately I Have Been Too Wrapped Up"
	"At the Lawn Party"
	"Forgive Me, But This Is Just a Smear of Purple"
Prairie Schooner:	"Dream: Catching the Air"
	"Apples"
Roanoke Review:	"Music of the Hands"
South Florida Poetry Review:	"Coventry Cathedral"
Sun Dog:	"The Aura"
	"Baiting My Hook, I Try Again"
Visions:	"From the Cloister, Saint-Rémy"
	"In the Hills of Les Baux"
Welter:	"The Crèche Dolls"
Wind/Literary Journal:	"Touch"

"Lately I Have Been Too Wrapped Up" also appears in the *Anthology of Magazine Verse & Yearbook of American Poetry (1985)*.

"Donna Bruna" was originally published in *Day Tonight/Night Today* before it was anthologized in *Montpelier Plus 4*.

Preface

As the reader will quickly discover, Carolyn Kreiter-Kurylo passionately loves the visual arts. In the first pages of *Contrary Visions* we encounter work by Piero Manzoni, Leonardo da Vinci, Vincent Van Gogh, and Marcel Duchamp, so that we are immediately aware of the painterly eye which informs all of this poet's work. She does not presume to tell us what the artist intended ("the artist intended nothing of this") or pedantically walk us through each detail of a canvas ("there is no end to what the artist holds in abeyance"). Instead, the intensity and care with which she sees is reflected in the tactile language she uses to capture moments of seeing—moments of being, for it is at those times when the artist makes, the observer responds, and the figures of a landscape enter the created world, that the poet is most vibrantly alive.

The poems tell us that Kreiter-Kurylo is a visual artist, a musician, a traveler, and teacher. Here is a poet who delights in texture, in harmony and patterned discord, in strangeness, history, memory, and the resilience of things humankind has made with energy and imagination. She can move from the edgy, agitated rhythms of "Nude Descending in All Directions," with its jazzy dadaist vocabulary—gadji beri bimba glandridi:—to the somber, trance-like sensuality of her sestina, "The Waters of Bath." When she writes of the creative process, she does so with a special sense of the way "sometimes in the middle of a painting the little things lose control." A similar quality of quiet daring is at work in the world outside the studio: in one poem, despondent, pacing in inner darkness, she climbs a tree from which she sees a blind woman, an "orphan surrounded by stray birds," circling in moonlight until the woman's cane strikes a familiar sidewalk; in another, "piddling the day away" fishing, she has a vision of colossal marionettes feeding the world. I'm inclined to believe her when she says, "Recently I climbed to the roof and shouted poems at the neighbors."

"Without Contraries is no progression," Blake tells us in *The Marriage of Heaven and Hell*. "Attraction and Repulsion, Reason and Energy, Love and Hate are necessary to Human existence." It is in this Blakean sense of Contraries—the dynamic, constructive opposition of equally true alternatives that lose validity without their counterparts—that Carolyn Kreiter-Kurylo titles her first book *Contrary Visions*. As the author puts it in her poem about the Mathematical Bridge at Cambridge, "the strength of the bridge [is] dependent on the strains." So there is silence and darkness here, as well as sound and light. The people in a number of these poems are deaf or blind or infirm, but the poet knows the world is no less various and intense when the eye is lightless or the ear mute, and she intuits how the senses may complement and supplement each other. In "Touch," for example, a deaf boy daydreams in late afternoon sunlight and tends a record player for his companion, an old woman who knits to the rhythms of *Die Meistersinger* ("each loop catching the air"), something, perhaps, for him.

Another kind of blindness afflicts the sighted: a self-serving, privileged ignorance Blake would have identified with Negation. More than once Kreiter-Kurylo tweaks the narrow and imperceptive "with their yardstick opinions" and "arsenic green touchstones." In "The Replica," one of the poems I most admire, she takes us to the Royal House of Dolls, a museum of anti-art in which the techically perfect, flawlessly ordered doll house is no more than "clever"—a diminutive monument to self-indulgence and a miniature mausoleum closed off even from its dolls. That kind of failure to engage with blemished, messy humanity makes Kreiter-Kurylo wake up angry and pound clay into fists. It sends her, "a woman who all her life has felt the need to connect," out to read poetry to the homeless and take her love of the arts—and a gentle self-mockery—into nursing homes and mental hospitals. Such reaching out, she implies, may be all we have against that other blindness, with "its marble and polished granite burning into the sky" and its cool, numb infatuation with destruction.

Despite its umbers and chiaroscuro, despite the way it leans into darker content, *Contrary Visions* is a book filled with praise. Throughout its pages "light lifts," "light carries," and even the fire of nuclear apocalypse is seen as "a terrifying ascent." The word "praise" orginally meant to price, to set a value upon and esteem, then later to proclaim, to speak highly of. What art does best, of course, is praise itself. Carolyn Kreiter-Kurylo's poems proclaim the beauty and abundance of this world—of memory, history, art and music, of outcasts and exemplars and the fragile, natural economies they inhabit—and as they do so, quietly they celebrate themselves. They are their own best source of wonder, and I hope her readers will value them as I do.

Peter Klappert
George Mason University

I. CONTRARY VISIONS

Contrary Visions in the Gallery, *White on White*

. . . just a white surface that is simply
a white surface and nothing else.
                    Piero Manzoni

The child in the paisley frock remembers
the terrible storm, how her father saved
her, how suddenly the white winds came.
Stepping forward, she folds her hands
intently into a gesture of peace
like the dove, before her, darkening
the surface halfway across the canvas.

Beside her, two mystics vow
this is not the coming of light
or white blossoms at the hands of God,
but a ceremonial stone that brings calm
to any man, if only he will embrace it.

Whereas the artist intended nothing
of this, no more than a white surface,
the lilies I remember turn back years,
and I am a small child again,

comprehending the emptiness of white
offerings, their incantations cold
beside the burial ground. I am moved
by this stillness, by the beguiling white
canvas holding just enough light
to enfold this darkness, this grief.

Donna Bruna

—after Leonardo da Vinci's *Mona Lisa,* 1503-05

The enigma seems tied in with the landscape behind her.

What is your secret, donna bruna?
The countryside pulls greens of a lake
into the corners of your mouth.
The light hovers there, and it matters
that the road behind you spirals,
tapers off toward the west,
that a bridge softens curiously
against the deep curve of your back.

How calmly you accept this condition,
one hand crossing the other, light caught
forever in the folds of skin, caught
in the lunar precipices beyond.

                    *

The air clouds with mist,
and the landscape changes
to Florentine streets
where a woman smiles desperately,

5

radiant creature locked in a pose,
the artist painting
at the end of a road.

Femina scura, he should let you go.
The light vanishes from skies.
Your eyes fill with years.

                    *

Four centuries, and your eyes,
donna bruna, as intense
as the day the artist leaned
you against the studio wall,
your shadow cast upon the floor.

He should let you go.
Already, fog crosses the lake,
rising toward the veiled sky,
toward a woman running
over luminous hills
where the wind passes over
like a crazed bird, calling
no need, no need to turn back now.

From the Cloister, Saint Rémy

Only when I am working in front
of my easel do I still feel
some life . . . .
        Vincent Van Gogh, Saint-Rémy asylum

. . . Their letters and gifts
are treacherous signs.
                    When Gauguin sends me
paintings, I struggle with demons.
I hear voices in fields
where wooden crosses twist
heavenward, where precipitous cliffs
rise.
                    And Bernard,
who professes to paint
from memory, produces nothing
more than creatures without pain,
saints without bones. I warn you,
Theo, these men deceive us.
Their accusations are wrong. I am not
an abstract painter. You must give them
no support.

I am weary.
My mind wanders steadily.
Sometimes I see chasms of fire, sometimes
a sky in flames. When the pain enters
my head, it is always the same
undulating motion.
                    After a seizure,
they tell me I have kicked
Poulet in the belly, or fallen
beneath barred windows, vials
of turpentine in my hands.

And the one who tries to poison me?
There is something quick
in his eyes. He follows
me through gardens. I know
he is there, a twisted figure
watching me paint. I hear him
whisper: *You are not one of us.*
You are a lowly peasant.
Again and again, the same voice.
                          I must leave
the asylum. I will return
to Holland, to its wheat fields
and rich earth. You must take
me with you, Theo. I will paint
in the open air.

Crows over the Fields of Auvers

. . . the truth is, we can only
make our pictures speak.
> *Vincent Van Gogh, from a letter found*
> *on his body after his suicide, July 1890,*
> *Auvers*

I.
I have been to Auvers
to study the flight of crows
who surely carry pain
in their blood. Today,
feeling the movement
of wheat, they caw a wild
song and with an airiness
that belongs to the wind,
fly low over a patch of earth
in a frenzied dance.

II.
Three is a sacred number.
To this Dutchman, three
meant dirt roads leading
nowhere, crows rising
from horizon toward a space

he chose for death.
He desired light, light
to make his pictures speak.
But unaccustomed to the sun,
he applied violence to the sky,
to the triangular formation
of birds, then stepping back,
with the spirit of a madman
counted to himself
and pulled the trigger.

III.
Now, in the cornfields of Auvers
the air turns warm black
with the progression of crows.
How peaceful, watching
their calm, determined flight
toward the lonely stone.
Cawing as they did years ago,
they call to him one last time
before rising out of golden grasses
and entering a dark blue sky.
All morning the sky deepens,
resuming the unrest below.

Nude Descending in All Directions

for Marcel Duchamp

Strip her bare.
Swirl her four dimensions
down those stairs stark
naked. She's just another sex cylinder
up your sleeve. Another blown
fuse in your paints.

You call her revolutionary,
rolling her frame like she's some cause
célèbre?
I call her
just another dame gone completely
anti-bourgeois, another one of your
tin lizzies, twitching
her petunia-pink saddlebags.

She's got *some* high-class itch,
wiggling her dimensions
into anti-art,
into the promised land of Arp
where he who eats Arp eggs

dies, and a single issue of *Rongwrong* prints
her name on a bottle rack
and calls it art.
                                    She moves you
into a land where everything's
pataphysics to bruitism,
where blue nudes wiggle their dreams loose,
where Mona Lisa giggles
and exits from the wall
when a readymade coat rack trips
your nude.

        She's balmy, this dame
who shimmy-shakes a wattlebird.
She wiggles out of duck eggs
into Dada.
                    Dada's everything pickaninny
black to mousse green.
Dada's gadji beri bimba glandridi:
your dame sounding off, popping
rhinoceroses again,
roaring 147
loud times.
        Dada's twittering
bird talk
with a red-breasted goose
like a king of the parallelopipedonists.
                    Dada's another chef d'oeuvre
that's hung around forty years,
waiting for an exhibit
on the moon.
                            You stripped
your nude bare for this?

Painting Poppies
near Arles

Poppies have a way
of barely moving
against soil, tilled
south of Arles.
A peasant, stooping
over red earth,
lays down her basket
to notice.

I pick up white:
a dove—several of them
fly north, their shadows
pearl gray.

You said, *It is never easy*
to paint poppies that bloom
crimson near Arles. You must wait
for the moment their color settles
in the viridine fields.

From the landscape
I select one scene
so delicate

rows of blossoms
stand perfectly still.

Beneath shadows
I apply blue,
then red, catching
unawares the old woman
intently gathering silence.

In the Bois de Vincennes, Paris

The rain holds its breath
in the Bois de Vincennes.

On a deserted path a woman
calls to her children:

*Dépêchez-vous. Le ciel pleut,
mes petits chéris.* Young,

with the faces of dawn, they cling
to her skirt, cling to the voice

of an angel as I do years later
waking to memory, knowing that today

I will write out of prayer,
and there will be no loneliness.

Other Possibilities

So this is Innsbruck, the old man whispers,
lifting his arms to embrace ornate churches,

their domes golden as the roof of that balcony
in the open square. Before a cathedral

riddled with bullet holes, he kneels
and crosses himself. He does not like

to think about war, his wife lighting
candles whenever he went away. Goethe said

the most sure and precious instrument
is the human eye. The man looks up

toward the sun painting the bullet holes
silver and beyond that, into windows

catching the playful rays. You can tell
by the way his eyes shine that he is dreaming,

small white birds dancing over him, covering
his shoulders with delicate feathers.

Alone, he returns to his room,
the bulb above the bed burning

with dignity, playing back
the details again and again.

Coventry Cathedral

—reduced to ruins by fire
bombs, November 14, 1940

There are some things we do not care
to remember: frail walls, frail

windows, scarred and stained, no
roof to contain their emptiness.

But the men of Coventry, when
their cathedral fell, persisted

and rose on the day after.
From charred beams they built

a cross before the ribs
of an altar where a light

still burns and lets nothing go.
For as long as the weather holds,

I will study these walls.
A sparrow drifts through

an open frame, nearly grazes
the edges, irregular, worn.

I would like to cradle this bird
in my palms. She is content

to build her home among ruins.
Bathing in air, she sings now.

Sun floods the remains, finds
this spirit alert among stones.

In winter, in a hard wind,
if the nest falls down

to a tattered heap, I will shape
a cross from the twigs, then lift

my creation to the highest wall
where there could be no finer light.

The Replica

No dolls live here. They do not walk
these palatial halls and chambers,
nor do they read. A shame . . .
      David Jeffery, "Royal House for Dolls"

For there are miniature books bound in leather,
a garden pergola, its trellis: a musical stave
carved deeply in an arched ceiling. And you,

moved by this pleasure, count
each rose, each blossom tilted
back, angled as a full note on the stave.

A comfort, the way you remember summer
flowers as a blessing, each petal tipped in a cream
or gold: I imagine a sonatina, the melody, long-held,

filling the royal house. There is a charm
about smallness, the way things take on dimensions
once reduced in size. Delighted, you stop

where orange tiger lilies, fuchsias, a ring
of toadstools grow in a garden so small
you take in the relationship of color

at a glance, while I remember years ago
the hunger in a man's eyes, how his blemishes,
inseparable from life, did not disappear

even in death. How peaceful,
looking now into every room at once, no flaws,
the illusion from a craftsman's hand, clever,

each reproduction flawless on a smaller scale.
A shame: to isolate this house
from the dolls, who stare

out of glass cases in the outer vestibule,
whose eyes hold no light, lids
that will not close. I remember you looked

at the dolls, I waited, but the light
would not charm their features, the proportion
on a larger scale, less definitive, inexact.

Even then, I saw the man's face, the scars
he carried from birth, the emptiness
of another house.

I look at the arched ceiling: each rose, a note
filling the silence, and a light
that will not turn this darkness away.

The Mathematical Bridge, Cambridge

A country sky, laced in orange, low-hanging
willows, and a bridge, russet-colored,
move light casually across the River Cam.

I wake in another country, the absence
of color startling, the room: a lattice
of light and shade, falling

across the wooden floor. Against the wall
stone turrets rise, their silhouettes granite
in a painting where a patchwork of red,

the fabled bridge in the foreground,
links a medieval garden to a brick alcove.
The light settles where the beams interlock,

and I am by the bridge again, by a chapel
where a stained-glass window lifts
blue into a strand, one thin line

crossing the glass the way a thread
rests against embroidered cloth.
I enter the chapel, a woman

who all her life has felt the need
to connect, who reaches out,
lights a candle, the glow entering

the chancel, breaking the coldness
of the evening air. The flame
angles into night, its strength

contained in the way the light lifts
out of darkness. This moment carries me
back to the last time I saw spring

touch the earth, to the place
where country lights brightened,
and I watched an island

of fire, the tips of calla lilies
holding sun, their petals: prisms
separating white into infinite facets.

The complexity, filament by filament,
dims from view where I lie
years later knowing this too

will interlock with time. I look
at the painting, the strength of the bridge
dependent on the strains, each wooden beam

locked in place, the river,
illuminated, still moving this design
through time even as it did years ago.

Touching a Stained-Glass Window in Gloucester Cathedral

for Eddie

Blind boy, I could be particular
and tell you how the design is made,

how faces, folds of drapery
are drawn, then baked in kilns

to flux the paint to the surface.
But how much truer to run

your fingers over colors, to say:
yellow, the imperial crown warms

your palms. Blue, cool fire
of a scepter calms your spirit.

Touch scarlet to understand anger:
not the red of robes that sparkle

with jewels, but flames that angle
and lash through a slate sky.

Feel the power of black where lead
strips give strength to the panes.

Fill your own darkness with soft
winds that rise from the sea, whitecaps

warm as milk lapping your skin.
Let the waves flow to you. Take them

into your heart where everything's
aglow with color and light.

The Peasant Woman above Tarifa

The shadow is bluest when the body
that casts it has vanished.
                    Rafael Alberti

Without warning she appears
in coastal hills, sea winds
blowing, no trees to calm
the land that sweeps like a luminous
shadow under the strait and into
the foothills of another country.

Clearly she has come for flowers,
gathering cluster upon cluster,
her apron swollen, overflowing.
Spanish lace for the children,
she marvels, then loosens
her blouse, uncovering a pendant,
circular, ornate. For a long
time she twirls the necklace
in the sun, and it shimmers.

Light blue, color of mist,
translucent, a Mediterranean moon—

it blues in the eyes of her children
when she returns home, covering
the table with rustling blossoms.

And when she reads to them,
it flutters, a seabird longing
for the slopes above Tarifa
where it would rinse in the light
this woman left behind, vanishing
into town, her shadow blue,
the earth bluer.

From a Café Window, Tangier

All morning there are suffering women,
a large flaming light, and an artist

sketching figures unaware
of his bold, deft strokes.

You can tell by the way he rocks
their bodies to and fro that the women

are conscious of the sea below.
Stooped over, they are washing

dishes in buckets of water,
the walls of the tenement building

doleful and flat, while the sun
rises toward the center of the sky

and rests. There is no end to what
the artist holds in abeyance,

all trace of human spirit gone,
the sky filled with a false brilliance.

The air grows cold, the stillness
broken by the women disappearing.

From a café window, I watch mist
cover them like a shroud

and in the distance, the artist
barely visible, painting by the sea.

Buttoning my coat to the wind,
I walk the narrow streets for hours

before returning to the studio to add
dark gray to a canvas, a solitary figure

coming into view and before him,
the waves reaching for the shore.

20th Century Studio Scene

All around
critics are taking their green frowns
off in public,
carping like Momus
with the same rood standards
he bared, laying
his breasts bare.

Oh, it's no different in here
when they come, tongue-lashing
like ill-humored pedants
on all fours.
With their yardstick opinions,
with their arsenic-green touchstones,
they come, walking
like pokes of air,
bantering just opposite
my public opinion
in an asymmetrical production
they color each time,
emptying
vinegar
in public.

Lately I Have Been Too Wrapped Up

in things, new job, new books,
new paints for the canvas, to let
the thoughts go until they settle

on something startling: this world,
for example, how it might be
otherwise if there were no colors,

if what came to us as the sea
were not blue, but a series of lines
you had to shape into swirling waves

to understand their essence.
I would cut fishline, tape it
to glass, then as a child might,

look through the surface
to the bottom. There would be Venice,
mosaic-goddess of the world,

found hundreds of years from now
at the bottom of the sea,
and in St. Mark's Square: a cathedral,

its walls and ceiling lined with stones,
faceted, ornamental stones in the shape
of Byzantine heroes. I would paint

the mosaics with water, let the Adriatic
Sea lap over their frosted surfaces.
On a day such as this, I do not need

to know colors to appreciate the property
of things. I can take a piece of string,
draw a basilica, look through its roof

to the inner walls where figures
touch one another and come to life
without the sun that lies

at the center of things
waiting to come to us
as coral, yellow, blue, or gold.

II. RITUALS

Rituals

A woman of the fields
stands watchful
in the night, lifting
her hands, the fruit
between them sweet
in an unspoken ritual.
The light rises for her.
Flowers glisten at her feet.

*

By morning there is
love in the woman's voice.
Planting seeds, she hums,
then bathes her hands
in soil while the wind
sings back.

*

A man points to the sun,
the moon, scratches pictures
on the earth floor.
The woman kneels beside
him. Words come

together, gradually
with understanding.

*

Their shadows become
one where they sleep
in an open field.
In the perfect light
they know their bodies
shape another, that he
will be like them.

*

The child does not speak.
He does not need to speak.
The man and woman sing.
And the child stands
in the center
of all light.

The Enchantress

Tanya, seducer of wolves, you enter
their wombs with sticks. You lighten
burdens of years in a revelry
we worship in dreams. We listen

as you suck pleasure from breasts. Pagan
woman, we watch you in thickets, your palms
calm as you gather and caress
priceless herbs. They blossom in your arms.

We follow you down paths beneath a canyon
sun, our bodies strengthened by your touch.
"Clutch the jagged ends of sticks," you whisper.
"Others before you have learned this much."

Our fingers, stretched out like talons, fondle
small teats. Warmth rushes into our throats.
Coats of hair linger on our tongues.
"Young women," you murmur, "float

along rivers. Lure men into your lair.
Bear and blossom an ageless gift: your song
among reefs swelling, slender women, your power
over men rising sweet and strong."

Fire

The age of the waters ended in a flood,
that of earth with an earthquake, of air
with a wind, and the present will be
destroyed by flame.
      Fernando de Alva Ixtlilxochitl

I.
Lightning craves the sap of a tree.
I am not talking of an innocent flash
above earth or of a radiant glow
that polishes the sky, but of a fire
spinning near the center of the tree
and lifting. What a terrifying ascent:
the juniper in a berth of smoke rising.

II.
And I am thinking of a young girl
who does not hear the echo of fire
along the forest floor. She is playing
a child's game, watching the milk
of the sky pale in this afternoon sun,
and the flames burning near
have not yet reached her.

III.
Listen. A miller is grinding
late today. Frightful sounds:
stone upon stone, flames licking
the windows, filling
the mill with violet.

IV.
On a mountain a goldsmith listens
to villagers call him from dreams:
The fires you ignite will melt
golden trees; they will scorch
your heart. Watching him melt
the disfigured limbs of a bird,
I think of fire, no one
rising out of ruins.

The Waters of Bath

*As early as the first century A.D., the townspeople of Bath,
England, worshiped Sulis, the goddess of healing, and in her
honor built a temple near the center of their city. On the out-
skirts, they buried those for whom the cure was not a success.
The youngest failure was Successa Petronia, a traveler from
Rome. Today visitors follow the ancients, throwing offerings
into the springs, hoping the gods will favor them.*
  —*Edited from Barry Cunliffe,* The Roman Baths

The waters of Bath did not cure
Successa Petronia. I uncover an urn
buried in a sacred spring,
beside it, several Bathstone
caskets and an engraved tablet: *The waters
did not heal these visitors to Bath—the ones*

*who traveled from Roman temples, the ones
who prayed to Sulis for a cure.*
The steaming waters
fill the bronze urn
as my fingers graze a headstone
overturned beneath the spring.

Who has concealed this spring,
this sacrificial font, and the ones

buried here? I pick up a carved carnelian stone—
the portrait of Sulis, goddess of the cure,
and a bronze inscription: *Whoever removes the urn*
from my temple shall become liquid as the waters.

Successa Petronia bathed in waters
near the altar of the Principal Spring.
From the chambers of Sulis, she carried the waters
    in the sculptured urn
back through the basilica to the ones
who waited for a cure.
Huddled behind stone

pillars near a limestone
quarry, foreign visitors prayed as Successa
    blessed the waters
she offered as a cure.
Young women performed rituals beside a nearby spring
while the older ones
knelt to drink waters from the urn.

Sulis fled from the temple in search of the stolen urn.
Clutching the carnelian stone,
she cursed Successa and the ones
she later buried here, but the goddess never found
    her urn concealed beneath the waters
of the sacred spring.
I lift the urn and the portrait of the goddess of the cure.

By the sacred spring, I offer this urn
to Successa, its healing waters as a cure.
To the ones Sulis turned away, I offer
    this carved carnelian stone.

In the Hills of Les Baux

Friends, you did not care
to climb the hills to Les Baux.

So alone, I take in this view:
clear skies to the south

and beneath them Arles,
Saintes-Maries-de-la-Mer.

Here the troubadours found
the source of words, sang

warm nights to women.
Their homes in ruins

glow in the Provence moon
while music pours from stars,

dreamers in love with this city,
its castle walls floating.

Poets, wherever you rest,
sleep in this alluring light

as I will sleep one day,
calmer for having climbed

these hills where the air
taken into the body

feels incandescent and once
released, turns to song.

Earth Mothers

From the thorn bush engraved for the goddess of quarrels
From the lavender cloaks and Egyptian crypts
From the bowels of serpents devoured in clump grass
I rise and drink the blood of Mimir

I drink vultures from the desert sun
I drink hundred-headed creatures, the barrens of Paros
I drink long-curved knives and carmine silk
I lift the twin rivers and drink

I lift spindles weaving labyrinths, my hair
I lift roots plucking harps, my fingers
I lift ash raining over Estonia
I lift the earth mothers who call *Volga!*

They drink, calling *Asgard!*
They drink, calling *Cigarren!*
They call *Ymir!* in the tongues of men

Ja, moder, the chariots
Ja, mutter, the swords
Oui, ma mère, the flames
I rise on the tongues of men,

chanting *tara brooch* in the goat's tongue

chanting *Hindu panch*, the cow's tongue
chanting *yama kiosk*, the wolves' tongue
chanting *miriska*
      miriska
      miriska

until Russians chant *balalaika*
until Hebrews chant *tussilage*
until I rise on pools of blood
wailing *ma mère*
      ma mère
      ma mère

In the Plaza of America, Seville

All day the air fills with scent
of orange, lotus and pecan.
Beyond palms, a wanderer sings,
pigeons scatter, their wings
harmonious, alert.
It is dusk, and in the plaza
I am again the child
who tossed pennies in a pool,
laughter floating into memories
of castanets and flamencos.
The moon turns, air-drunk,
toward pergolas heady
in the spring heat.
I enter the ritual:
horse-drawn carts
pass toward *La Maestranza*,
Sevillians drink fino.
Outside a dance hall
alive with strumming,
I become the thrumming
of the strings. My mother
plucks a lute. I rock
on the porch swing

in the shadows of Virginia
while she hums a Spanish tune
that drifts overseas
and dissolves in the warm
winds of this country.

Spell of Moon and Maple

How is it that the tree
keeps on shining,   *Circling*
its tattered skin   *the tree*
torn by dark mouths   *three times,*
gnawing in a hard wind?

How is it that the tree,   *wander*
worn and alone, reaches   *into a deep,*
into the sky and scatters   *blustery*
October's rubies
over the graying earth?   *night.*

The jewels hold fast
to the bare, flat roots   *Let*
as though feeding hungrily   *the full moon*
on the soul of a tree.   *drop*

Beneath traces of scarlet clouds
fingering the branches,   *from the sky.*
I bend down to gather   *Collect*
pieces of the tree's heart
for my children.

Far from where they sleep,
I rub my fingers over   *the tree's heart.*

the smooth bark.
In the night's stillness
the tree takes the moon   *The children's eyes*

into its arms and spangles   *no longer*
the children's dreams.   *fear the night.*

A Deaf Woman
Longs to Be
among the Waters

To discover an aura
so grand
the sea emits
an imposing blue sound.

To sculpt mosaic waves
into birds,
fling them into flight:
dumb flourishes of song.

To swim into a lake's heart
where the cadence
of fish startles the deep;
to shelter minnows

in the palms, their dartings:
glissades.
To move toward the shore
where a heron answers

her young. To be that heron
strumming
the air, a choir
embroidered in her singing.

Take This on Authority

When the last cloud leaves
nothing behind—no
history, no trace of error, no
basilica to shelter a man—
a hymn, as lonely as any,
will rise out of canyons
and at great heights
sing to every particle, to
every hint of light along the way.
In a temple, in another
universe, listeners will
bow down chanting.

III.   GIFTS

Baiting My Hook,
I Try Again

Just piddling the day away,
my sister says, letting her line
drop to the bottom. I let
my line down, not caring
if the fish bite, figuring
This sure is country living.
Agreeable. Slow. I look back
toward the bridge where storm
clouds gather, and beneath them
rain grays the sky. A sharp
tug on the line, and I reel
in a universe where colors
prevail, where clouds redden
with lightning, a tiny ship fighting
the sea, its bold masts crimson.
Wind rises, and I want
to leave this boat, climb
to the world's roof, paint
dilapidated buildings topaz,
punctuate their pallid shadows.
In this world I want colossal
strings to descend from trees.
Pull one: peaches fall. Another,

plums, dazzling, plump.
I want more strings to fall
from the arms of puppets.
How quickly they gather
baskets for the poor,
parade through India, China,
streets of Africa, hungry
mouths dancing with fruit.
Wine flows into the Ganges, Yangtze,
and Niger, where thousands fill
buckets with the ruby liquid.
Waves slap the boat, and I
climb down from this world.
Reeling in my line, I slide
the worm's frayed skin
from the hook, the fish gone.
This minute the sky opens up.
In my mind, I pull a string
and color the earth for miles
with mulberry light.

Apples

Today I'm thinking of apples,
a country kitchen, the smell

of pie cooling in the late
summer air. Let's say

it's evening, the hour
when anything's possible.

A small girl in a hammock
dreams of lightning: *poor will,*

poor will, a horse's whinny
in the air. She wakes

to a wind, apples thrown
to the earth: succulent globes

that she rubs and rubs
until the world shines.

I'd like to say this happened
the first time a woman plucked

an apple and saw it as good.
I'd like to say she took the juices

of berries and painted a still
life that comes alive tonight

in the palms of a child,
the ripest fruit tilted

toward the light, ageless
and holding on.

The Aura

In the works of man as in those of nature,
it is the intention which is chiefly worth
studying.
                    Goethe

How intently she guides her brush
hour after hour, the strokes twisting
into flames, some turning crimson,
some sullen against a night sky.
Later, she stands back, stares
at the canvas, not a trace of aura
lifting, the stars random, indistinct.

In the fullness of the design,
she adds hydrangeas to the sky,
blue against half-light, their petals
formed by hands certain of their control.
She lifts darkness into soft winds
before stepping back to study
the hydrangeas, the way they carry light
casually into leaves, how they fold
the air back on a dome of color moving
silence even now into the room.
Look closely. It is the sign
she has waited for, nearly audible,
distinct, and still lifting.

The Crèche Dolls

Two crèche dolls and this urge
to lie down beside them
dressed in a thin gown.
And the light overhead
out of all control—
in their eyes, small
white crosses.

It is warm where I stand
in a circle of stars, storm
clouds parting, though no one
sees them or hears me
carve wood: the chink, chink
lost to attendant winds
longing themselves
for the company of dolls.
The winds lean over
and touch them as I would
clay or stone. Speaking
their own language, they turn
the dolls gracefully
toward the sky.

On the piazza I place the third
doll beside the others,
the light lifting, leaving
traces of gold over their bodies
stretched out like offerings.

What You Hear in a Studio

Sometimes in the middle of a painting
the little things lose control: a stroke
of gray leans into a country barn
like smoke, or one line chases another
along city streets, swerves
left into a fence post
you suddenly put there.

You begin again: this time you imagine
a hawk's cry, ready to paint
his path across the cool green.
A fortunate accident, you whisper
as the sound enters, as moonlight
descends louder through the dark leaves
to surround you in the moment
you listen for.

To Walk Out on Three Musicians

There they were at the opening:
three men
disguised, situating
themselves in the metallic paint,
composing a collage,
as if they had Bach's ear
for polyphony on stage.

They stood rigid,
Monk, Harlequin, and Pierrot,
or perhaps they would have
played for us
after all.

With their jigsaw
of harlequin costumes and masks,
with their cubism on a sheet
of soundless canvas,
they robbed us, deceived us
with a masque
of mute concertina.

Bach would have also walked out, Picasso,
if he had seen those
three masked men

holding up the performance
in silence.

He would have walked right out.
Your diamond-suited
cylinders and cubes
forgot the geometry of sound,
as if his counterpoint were a lie.

Forgive Me, But This Is Just a Smear of Purple

he says and walks away from my painting,
a young man smug as the cinereous skies

of Long Island where a drab rain falls
and gives seed to nothing. *What happens*

to him does not matter, I tell myself
admiring the canvas. Picking up a brush,

I enliven the countryside: lavender
fields, cedars, a grove of oak trees

turning orchid as moonlight cloaks
the stars. I wait for a fine,

raking light to clear an opening
in the mist, to pave my way

to the hills where hundreds of stones
hold onto the moon—clean, bleached,

pearly stones that sweep up to greet
the light. Striking a match,

I read my name on a headstone
while the Long Islander chisels

today's date. The blow of steel
against stone wakes me from the vision.

Though it's happened before,
I've come to accept this illusion

as a price to pay for altering
the world so that an ordinary

scene will burn with clarity
and in the palest light, catch fire.

Dream: Catching the Air

I.
I watch them lower you.
Each time in the night's
thin hour, you tremble.
Your face, its gaze
once cold under lamplight,
struggles out of a seizure.
You raise your mouth
and breathe back.

Staying long in my dream,
you breathe air
into the mouth laboring
over yours.
Out of a tremor,
you move, catching
air on your tongue
as if you might fill
your lungs.

II.
This morning I place iris
on the bedstand, watch
them turn velvet
as first light floods

your room. Our summers
were like this: opening
windows to mountains,
honeysuckle reaching us
through mist. Afternoons
we wrote on the porch
swing. Always before bed,
you read *Light in August*
or *Les Misérables.*
"What one man won't do
to another," you said resting
your head on the bedpost,
your voice steady.
Now each time you speak
to me in a dream, I wake,
my heart opening, and write
down your words.

III.
For years I go on recording.
This evening shadows
around me flicker, the house
dark. A candle illumines
your picture as a young
girl lying in a bed
of clover. Were you
dreaming, keeping
your mother alive
in sleep? I lean
my head against a chair's
back and doze off.
In a dream you rise
from the clover. Running
toward you, I extend

my arms, taking you in.
Again a seizure pulls
you down. You struggle
for air while moonlight
pours across the floor.
I wake wondering,
How long can we keep
the dead alive this way?
Until the skies darken,
the stars seem to say.
All these years you have
done it so well.

The Blind Woman, 1967

I grew old at twenty. The war tugged
at my spirit, Mother drowned in her own fluid,
and I retreated to my room to think of islands

and wildflowers. One evening I wandered
to a grove, climbed sprawling branches,
let the vertiginous wind braid my hair.

I paced in a treehouse, latticed with haze,
until my eyes fell on a stranger groping
through darkness, the rap of her cane

audible in the wind. The sidewalk's curve
interrupted her journey. Lost on the lawn,
she tapped the ground for a familiar clink,

this orphaned figure surrounded by stray birds.
Circling through moonlight, she steadied
her stance, the balmy air lowered a shroud,

and I was awed by her struggle.
She struck the sidewalk while shooing
away pigeons, then continued her journey

into the beguiling night. I cannot
forget those eyes, closed as in praise.
I held onto the moon as it found

the spot that had swallowed her.
I wished her farewell, then stepped
back to light, to a field, luminescent.

The Concertos

The farm's calm this hour,
cerulean pond, distant hum
of a fan, flies circling
the apple trees and landing.
Lying down near the grove,
I let go of this day: warm
breeze full of great white
puffs of milkweed that take
me back to 1950. I am
four years old. Tchaikovsky
flows from the back parlor
up the stairs to the playroom
where I tap the floor
in keeping with the tempo.
Imagining fairies' laughter,
I sing all afternoon
while my mother plays on.

*

Closing my eyes tighter,
it's winter. I'm fifteen.
All day he sits by my side
repeating, *Mark the tempo.*
Let those fingers hurt.

Hour after hour, I do,
hoping the concertos will
soon lift into concerts.
A *street musician,* my mother
calls him the night he vanishes.

*

Opening my eyes, I watch
the sun slide along my fingers.
A light breeze covers the earth,
and I doze off long enough
to remember the melodies.
Time and again in a wish,
he comes back from the hills.
I stand before him with nothing
between us but the space his song
leaves, fading into half notes
through the hollows of trees.

Touch

The boy in the room does not hear
Die Meistersinger, though the rhythm
of the woodwinds touches an old woman
knitting next to him. Her fingers move
deliriously, each loop catching
the air: *Briskness everywhere,*
she marvels, but the child does not
take her words in. Perhaps he is
in an open field where music
as a wind-dance surrounds his body.
He stares so calmly into air's fullness.

The mastersingers take their leave,
but the woman does not notice
the needle lift from the record
or see the late afternoon sun
weave its warmth along her arms.
She is accustomed to darkness,
to the touch of a child's
hand, constant and assured,
wiping this stillness away.

A Former Teacher Said It Is Not Easy

Young and agreeable, I took up
my pen and wrote: *The poet
is like a cow giving birth
in distant fields.* Thinking
it silly, my teacher laughed,
and my classmates laughed,
and for a while that
was that for poetry.

Today, I hold up a picture
of animals feeding
and tell my students:
"There is something remarkable
in being able to fill
bodies with warmth
as these cows do."

No one says a word,
but the children stare
at the photograph as if
they see the child I was
running from school
to the barn where I curled

up next to a calf
and fell asleep
believing in shining
creatures, full-grown
and ready for pasture.

Proctoscopic
Humiliation

This morning I was in one of
those positions
I assume for my doctor:
kneeled over,
neck craned
     like a bad-tempered ostrich
lifting its prey.

I thought
the snow tires couldn't talk
back
but they did, those tires
that had kicked through snow
for me, bad-tempered
     like an ostrich
at 30 mph.

They pulled at my underweight
to let go.
     Goddamn you, tires.
You argued back
and trampled my dignity
right off that table

where I had perched
minutes ago
ready to tell my doctor
to go to hell.

At the Lawn Party

for Judy, undaunted by her blindness

On the lawn the cooling winds
startle a young woman,
a fine scent alerting her
that someone places a bowl
of fruit on the dinner tray.
It seems a long time
before melons, peaches, berries
warming in the sunlight
touch her lips, the spoon
skimming the surface
lazily, her eyes fragile
stars in the liquid.

Nearby, a man is singing to her.
Poised in her own darkness,
she listens as he defines
honeysuckle, elm, great cedar
trees with a voice that carries
her into a sea of clouds.

I am calmed by a woman who feels
the sweep of my hands as wind
blossoms along her shoulders,

her dignity certain in the way
she knows colors as rainbows.
And all I ask is that
with each spoonful of fruit
she takes into her body,
the rainbows go on
shining as they do now
in the light of her face.

Music of the Hands

for a deaf student teacher

All morning you've crafted words
that become *Moonlight Sonata*
while shadows stream across the floor.
I do not need to know you to praise
the way you speak, your hands curved
into sparrows, harmony gliding
from their mouths. Watching your arms
move like a maestro's, I know
you have something festive to say.
Wherever there are schools, perform
your music. Let your fingers
dance the mazurka's brisk step.
And for those who prefer the tempo
of jazz, play ragtime as you do
now in a wind that ignites
the eyes of children.

Sam's Accident

They say it's a big water leak.
Here I am with Sam. A mistake
in the first place: this crazy need

to be a good Samaritan.
Sam, an octogenarian,
peers down, checks his own water bag

as I fill the radiator,
pray for a small miracle or
two. Ninety-nine degrees. *Hot,*

I mouth aloud, the car's water
dripping out, Sam's bag much fuller.
Twelve miles to the nursing home, twelve,

I complain, cranking the old Ford.
Sam takes his time to climb aboard,
smiles as if he adores every

last bit of this trouble. I think
of his bag, filling to the brink.
All right. Let's say all hell breaks loose,

and Sam drowns in the damn liquid
unsanctified. Heaven forbid
it explodes in this air-tight car.

At eighty plus, I round the curve,
skid to a halt, suddenly swerve
into the path of six nurses,

waiting, arms akimbo, outside
the home. Sam disembarks, wide-eyed,
purified by the racy ride,

while I, heart and all, move away
from that eagle-eyed nurse, undismayed
when Sam's spray hits her square in the face.

For a Franciscan Brother

So you want to take your life—
three parallel slashes, *three,*
you said, one for you, your spirit,
and the Holy Father.

I remember months ago
you knelt in the Friary, vowed
to follow a life of chastity, poverty,
and humility. After the profession
a woman, moved by ceremony, honored
you with a replica of St. Francis.
You raised the wooden carving
so high that light from a stained-
glass enlivened the deep-set eyes
that seemed to plead for obedience.

My mind whirls back
to the '70s, you in the hospital
again and again, your disease cold
and relentless, pursuing you
even in remission.

This morning
you knelt by the bed to pray
for nourishment, your white gown

a thin shadow of yourself.
Outside, rain soaked the clothes-
line where a stiff breeze swallowed
a shirt and slacks, spun
them into spirited angels.

Tonight in a vision
I see you in a crowd of lepers,
epileptics, children extending
their arms to a religious: you,
in a Brother's habit, move
to the circle's center
like a proud animal. In full
light you shower their hearts
with prayers. The scene
dissolves into a solitary figure
preaching to birds.

Leaning over a sink,
I douse my cheeks and brow
with water before entering
the studio where I throw
lights onto a half-finished
statue. I encircle the piece
with my palms, carry it
to the work table, let
my fingers stroke the dark
robe, a thin rope coiled
around a delicate waist.

As I work, I remember
a basilica on Mount Subasio,
dozens of larks flocking
about the feet of a sculpted man

so proud he lifted his eyes
past the grayed and graying
roofs of Assisi into sky
close enough to touch.

Moving toward the table,
I breathe air into the figure.
Though the broken frame
starts to crumble, I steady
my hands and repair remnants
of a condemned body, then return
the sculpture to its resting place
among a gallery of characters.

      Half-asleep,
I watch the other figures
come alive, hoist the Brother
to their shoulders where he
breaks off a piece of sky,
consumes it and spirals
into the clouds, stars,
into white light
where someone told him
he would find a cure.

        1986

I Don't Know Why I
Wake Up Angry

at the young for pushing their mothers
and fathers into nursing homes, for letting
them die hunched over, penniless.

I sometimes walk by asylums repeating
care, care. Recently I climbed to the roof
and shouted poems at the neighbors.

Madwoman, they jeered, their eyes dark
holes in the air. Lately I have let
the blind keep the lilies I paint,

pounded clay into fists, struggled
to understand the slurred speech
of stroke victims. I have pushed air

into a woman's diseased lungs so she could
praise the prism she held in her hands.
I have run a blind woman's fingers

over Michelangelo's *David* so she would know
he is thinking of enemies, how to escape.
On her death bed, Mother whispered barely

audible strains, echoed this morning
in the rain's breath and years ago
in winds over the burial ground: *Care,*

care, she spoke into a mirror, knowing
the face that stared back would wrinkle
and offend. Last night at Second and D,

I read poetry to the homeless, watched
ladies from St. Elizabeths falter.
Mindless, they drifted toward the fields

portrayed in a poem, pretended to plant
seeds, then knelt in their own bleak
shadows to pray and pray for miracles.

Homeless on Independence Avenue

Who can say how long he will
lie here, spanning the grate
like an aging bridge clinging
to life? Six p.m., he claims
his territory, back turned
toward the Capitol dome,
toward Freedom flickering
in the weary sun. I look up
at a street light, the bulb
broken, slivers strewn
over the victim's coat.
The old man rises to his knees,
and in his lapel a tulip grows,
so bold it outlives the chill.
Steam from the grate enshrouds
the crimson beauty, then vanishes
into the tulip's mouth.
I cannot say how long
he kneels before my bus
pulls to the curb, and I climb
aboard. Riding on Independence,
I glance back on all I know

of this block. The Capitol
grows larger, and as I search
the pale walls, search
for stones that fade and chip,
the night lights open up
and disclose the city's ruins.

The Visiting Poet,
Washington, D.C.

No one below on the expansive lawn,
the streets a maze leading anywhere

this hour of night as you take in
the charm of this city, its marble

and polished granite burning into the sky.
The moon hangs low, every sound lost,

the air motionless where the bridges
cast silver over the river.

You wonder if the spell passes
through other cities, London, Amsterdam,

Rome, whether the wind settles
like light in another place and time.

Musing, you miss a siren's call,
never mind the cries of hookers

and addicts who do not see the moon,
who do not care. And what do you care,

recording the sights of this city?
Tomorrow you will rise to the podium

and recite your poems, drunkards
and bag ladies beyond the Great Hall

humming their songs, their bodies
pressed to the earth among the noble façades.

The Tidal Basin
Holds Time Still

in the monument's reflection.
A gentleman, cradling his daughter,

misses this, the amulets in her
eyes: moonstones she'll find

refulgent in her own children's eyes.
The monument wavers, casts a charm

on a young couple in the merry act
of loving this protean pool.

Time breathes loosely as they bathe
their feet and skim pebbles

across the rhythmic surface.
And what about the man and his daughter?

Do they think Time circles
the Basin, returns, and repeats

the pattern? The man gazes off,
perhaps into his mother's eyes,

into the eyes of every woman
who preceded her, back to the years

when the family came home to a meal
of potatoes and bread. Softly,

he whispers something German
to the child who asks her father

if he will live forever. This instant
a barrage of pebbles distorts

the child's words, the monument before
her disappearing into the depths.

Gifts

Tonight I bring you Camembert, Brie,
Port Salut, aged to soft yellows
from the hills of France. Delightful,

the way you fold these cheeses into spinach,
how they carry a buttery fragrance
outdoors where children lie, listening

to a wind, bells singing from the steeple
near the corner store. Imagine every evening
like this: counting stars until the sky

becomes a polished lamp. Charmed,
you notice lavender pulled in
from the garden, mounds swelling

to a lavish brown: a roomful of flowers
and breads. Marigolds, violets,
wild plum come to you, the moon.

The sudden smell of wine finds you
dressing flowers, their points
moist with a white as sweet as milk.

A pleasure, the way you fill the distance
with pastures, select the blackest cows
for cream. This is more than imagination:

the aroma of bread rising
about the kitchen, the Brie's
smooth skin gently darkening.

Mountains

For as long as I live, I will love
mountains rising out of villages,

holding onto sun, threading light.
I will love them on a country's

border stepping into wind, free
for miles. If someone mentions

the Himalayas or Kilimanjaro,
I will think of men

who have climbed those peaks,
touched the sky and turned

lovely as stone. A comfort,
not to think of death in the valleys,

sunlight pouring over plains,
giving back what is theirs.

May the snows come: it is
beautiful to love mountains,

to have lived in the sanctuary
of ancient slopes and felt mountains

glide into silence, to go on
loving them in words.

Notes

"Contrary Visions in the Gallery, *White on White*"

The epigraph, which expresses Italian painter Piero Manzoni's intention to rid his canvases of all symbolism and connotation, is printed here in its entirety: "a white that is not a polar landscape, not a material in evolution or a beautiful material, not a sensation or a symbol or anything else: just a white surface that is simply a white surface and nothing else." [From Herbert Read, *A Concise History of Modern Painting,* Oxford University Press, 1974, p. 308].

"Donna Bruna"

donna bruna: dark lady
femina scura: obscure woman

"From the Cloister, Saint-Rémy"

Vincent Van Gogh was confined for extreme depression during the last year of his life (1889-1890) to Saint-Rémy asylum, located near Arles in southern France. At this time he disagreed vehemently with painters Paul Gauguin and Emile Bernard about the aims of art. From *The Letters of Vincent Van Gogh,* edited by Mark Roskill (New York: Atheneum, 1970, p. 328): ". . . The thing is that I have worked this month in the olive groves, because they [Bernard and Gauguin, who had sent records of their recent work] have

99

maddened me with their Christs in the Garden, with nothing really observed. Of course, with me there is no question of doing anything from the Bible—and I have written to Bernard and Gauguin too that I considered that to think, not to dream, was our duty, so that I was astonished looking at their work that they had let themselves go so far. For Bernard has sent me photos of his canvases. The trouble about them is that they are sort of dream or nightmare—that they are erudite enough—you can see that it is someone who is mad on the primitives—but frankly the English Pre-Raphaelites did the thing much better . . . ."

Van Gogh and his beloved brother Theo corresponded on a weekly basis for nearly ten years (1880-1890). Their correspondence is preserved in *The Letters of Vincent Van Gogh.*

"Crows over the Fields of Auvers"

Vincent Van Gogh's painting, *Crows Over the Wheat Field,* completed shortly before the artist committed suicide in 1890, is the basis for this poem. Meyer Schapiro in *Vincent Van Gogh* (Doubleday & Company, Inc., 1890, p. 130) presents this description of the painting: "The singular format of the canvas is matched by the vista itself, a field opening out from the foreground by way of three diverging paths . . . these end blindly in the field or run out of the picture . . . . The blue sky and the yellow fields pull away from each other with disturbing violence; across their boundary, a flock of black crows advances toward the unsteady foreground."

"Nude Descending in All Directions"

This poem emerged after viewing Marcel Duchamp's painting *Nude Descending the Stairs.* Duchamp said about his painting: "It is an organization of kinetic elements, an expression of time and space through the abstract presentation of motion . . . ." (Herbert Read, *A Concise History of Modern Painting,* p. 113).

The aim of the Dada art movement was to shock the bourgeoisie—whom the Dadaists blamed for World War I—by breaking up conventional notions of art as Duchamp did in his reproduction of Mona Lisa with a moustache.

"In the Bois de Vincennes, Paris"

"*Dépêchez-vous. Le ciel pleut, mes petits chéris.*": "Hurry. It is raining, my little ones."

"The Replica"

The replica referred to in this poem is Queen Mary's Dolls' House presented to Queen Mary as a token of national goodwill. The Dolls' House is currently on display at Windsor Castle in England.

"The Mathematical Bridge, Cambridge"

The Mathematical Bridge, located at Cambridge University in England, was designed by Sir Isaac Newton and built in 1749-50. Held together by calculated strains with no nails or bolts to mar the russet-colored beams, the fabled bridge arcs across the River Cam linking the medieval brick buildings of Queens' College to the Back Greens.

"To Walk Out on Three Musicians"

Pablo Picasso's cubist composition, *Three Musicians* (1921), is the basis for this poem.

About the Author

Carolyn Kreiter-Kurylo was born in 1946 and grew up in Richmond and in the mountains of southwestern Virginia. A graduate of Mary Washington College, she received her M.Ed., M.A., and Doctor of Arts in Education degrees from George Mason University. A painter, sculptor, and poet, she currently works as a language arts and writing resource teacher for Fairfax County Public Schools and as an adjunct professor for George Mason University where she teaches graduate poetry courses to teachers. Her poems and articles on writing have appeared nationwide in such publications as *Antioch Review, English Journal, Poet Lore, Prairie Schooner, Mid-American Review, Wind, Anthology of Magazine Verse and Yearbook of American Poetry, The Writing Center Instructor*, and *The Journal of Teaching Writing*. She has received grants from both the Virginia Commission for the Arts and the Virginia Center for the Creative Arts to support poetry-in-the-schools programs. A finalist in the "Discovery"/*The Nation* poetry contest, she received recognition for quality research from the Virginia Educational Research Association for her doctoral dissertation, *Gathering Light: A Poet's Approach to Poetry Analysis*. Carolyn Kreiter-Kurylo lives outside of Washington, D.C., in Burke, Virginia.

Scripta humanistica

Directed by
BRUNO M. DAMIANI
The Catholic University of America
COMPREHENSIVE LIST OF PUBLICATIONS *

Forthcoming

* Carlo Di Maio, *Antifeminism in Selected Works of Enrique Jardiel Poncela.* $20.50
* Juan de Mena, *Coplas de los siete pecados mortales: Second and Third Continuations.* Ed. Gladys Rivera. $25.50
* Salvatore Calomino, *From Verse to Prose: The Barlaam and Josaphat Legend in Fifteenth-Century Germany.* $28.00
* Darlene Lorenz-González, *A Phonemic Description of the Andalusian Dialect Spoken in Almogía, Málaga — Spain.* $25.00
* Maricel Presilla, *The Politics of Death in the «Cantigas de Santa María.»* Preface by John E. Keller. Introduction by Norman F. Cantor. $27.50
* *Studies in Honor of Elias Rivers,* eds. Bruno M. Damiani and Ruth El Saffar. $25.00
* Godwin Okebaram Uwah, *Pirandellism and Samuel Beckett's Plays.* $28.00

BOOK ORDERS

* Clothbound. *All book orders,* except library orders, must be prepaid and addressed to **Scripta Humanistica**, 1383 Kersey Lane, Potomac, Maryland 20854. *Manuscripts* to be considered for publication should be sent to the same address.